Learn'Em Good

-Essay Writing-

Essay Writing Skills for Kids: Help Your Child Write Essays, Personal Narratives, Persuasive Expositions, Procedures, Reports, Descriptive Writing, Paragraphs, and Explanations

Stuart Ackerman MSc.Ed, B.A.

Learn'Em Good Publishing

www.LearnEmGoodBooks.com

Watch for the following Learn'Em Good books:

Learn'Em Good Writing
Learn'Em Good Math
Learn'Em Good Reading
Learn'Em Good Grammar
Learn'Em Good Homeschooling
Learn'Em Good Learning Disabilities
Learn'Em Good ADD/ADHD
Learn'Em Good Study Skills
Learn'Em Good Geometry
Learn'Em Good Fractions
Learn'Em Good Social Skills
Learn'Em Good Adventures of Peter Pan
Learn'Em Good Adventures of Pinocchio
Learn'Em Good 20,000 Leagues Under the Sea
Learn'Em Good Alice in Wonderland
Learn'Em Good A Journey to the Center of the Earth
Learn'Em Good Aladdin and the Wonderful Lamp
Learn'Em Good Around the World in Eighty Days
Learn'Em Good Doctor Dolittle
Learn'Em Good Frankenstein
Learn'Em Good Gulliver's Travels
Learn'Em Good Moby Dick
Learn'Em Good Tarzan of the Apes
Learn'Em Good The Adventures of Robin Hood
Learn'Em Good The Island of Doctor Moreau
Learn'Em Good The Second Jungle Book
Learn'Em Good The Swiss Family Robinson
Learn'Em Good The Three Musketeers

Learn'Em Good

Learn'Em Good The Time Machine
Learn'Em Good The Wonderful Wizard of Oz
Learn'Em Good Treasure Island
Learn'Em Good The Lost World

Table of Contents

More Writing Tips

Introduction

The ability to write is one of the most important skills you can impart to your child. Regardless of the future vocation your child chooses, he or she will require highly developed writing skills.

The ability to write is like riding a bike. That is, once your child can do it, it is his or hers forever.

There are several reasons why you should help your child to write at home:

1. Your child's grades in school will improve.
2. Your child will improve his or her self expression.
3. Your child will have a better chance getting a college or university degree.
4. Writing skills have a direct correlation to your child's future job success and socio-economic status.
5. Your family will spend quality time together.
6. Your child will have greater confidence in his or her writing and overall scholastic abilities.

When I refer to 'writing', I'm not restricting it to just a pencil and paper. Using a word processor or other technological tool require the same basic writing principles as to writing manually. What I am referring to, is the ability to convey thoughts onto a physical surface, construct sentences, paragraphs, ideas, and the mechanics of writing itself. Writing is more than putting words on paper. It is the final stage of 'thinking'.

Parents don't realize that they can have a major impact on their child's writing skills. I realize, as a teacher, that most parents are not familiar with the curriculum in their state or province (that's why I wrote this book). It is difficult for most parents to know how to properly format a paragraph, organize a report, or write an explanation. These types of writing are taught and assessed in the classroom. What parents can help their children with though, are the 'practical' writing skills that should be practiced at home.

This book is intended for students from grade 1-8. I have given you many ways to help your child write at home. I have provided the essential information to help your grade 1-8 child with any major essay writing assignment. I suggest that you read over the information for each type of writing assignment before helping your child. So, for example, let's assume that your child is planning on writing a personal narrative. I recommend that you first read about personal narratives before helping your child with the actual lesson in this book.

The grades indicated for each lesson in this book are simply guidelines. If your child is having difficulty or requires practice, he or she can try any lesson regardless of the grade level. It is strongly recommended that your child try the lesson that is in the lower grades before trying the lesson that is at your child's grade level.

Finally, all of the templates in this book can be photocopied for your personal use. I suggest that you copy them and not write in this book so that you can reuse the templates at a later date.

Good luck and Learn'Em Good!

Stuart Ackerman

Descriptive Writing

Descriptive Words

Descriptive words are the backbone for writing descriptive sentences, descriptive paragraphs, and descriptive essays.

When editing and proofreading a piece of writing, it is important to remove and change non-descriptive words to more descriptive ones.

Verbs
Verbs make sentences come alive. Verbs are action words that give movement to writing and allow the reader to visualize the action.

For example: *I was tired, so I* ***walked*** *to the door and* ***turned*** *the handle.*

We can change the verbs in this sentence so that it is becomes more descriptive by giving us a better picture.

For example: *I was exhausted, so I* ***staggered*** *to the door,* ***squeezed*** *the handle and* ***twisted*** *it to the right.*

Nouns
Common nouns such as *car, dog, tree,* and *man* aren't very descriptive. We can substitute these nouns with proper nouns such as *Toyota, Dalmatian, Maple*, and *Mr. Jones*. These nouns are specific and they let the reader visualize the writing more clearly.

Colorful Adjectives and Adverbs
Colorful adjectives and adverbs can make or break a piece of writing, especially a narrative. Adjectives and adverbs, also known as modifiers, can mean the difference between a non-descriptive and very descriptive piece of writing.

Example: *He walked through the forest and saw a bear.*

We can add adjectives and adverbs to paint a better picture of this scene.

He ***cautiously*** *walked through the* ***dark*** *forest and saw a* ***ferocious Grizzly*** *Bear.*

It is important for your child to first write his or her sentences, and then add in descriptive words. Your child should also be able to use a thesaurus. Try to purchase a child-friendly thesaurus for your child. Clearly focusing on detailed verbs, nouns, and modifiers will enhance and improve the quality of your (or your child's) writing.

Descriptive Writing – Forming Sentences Grades 1-4

When writing a **descriptive sentence**, you must create a clear picture of a thing or a person. It is important to write what you see, smell, taste, hear, and touch. This lets the reader understand and picture what you are writing about.

Look at the picture of a park and see how the chart is filled in.

What I can see.	–kids playing -a tree -grass -slide -kids sliding
What I can hear.	–laughing -birds chirping - the wind
What I can smell.	–fresh air
What I can taste.	- nothing
What I can touch.	–cold metal slide - soft grass -slippery slide

Now we can write sentences from our senses. Try to combine the dot jot notes into sentences.

1. I see kids laughing as they go down the slide.
2. The boy feels the cold metal slide as he climbs up to the top.
3. I can smell the fresh air and hear the wind.
4. I can hear birds chirping in the nearby tree.

Look at the picture of the beach. Fill in the chart. Remember to add detail.

What I can see.
What I can hear.
What I can smell.
What I can taste.
What I can touch.

Now we can write sentences from our senses. Try to combine the dot jot notes into sentences. <u>Have an adult help you and check your work.</u>

1.____

2.____

3.____

4.____

5.____

Answers will vary

Descriptive Words, Sentences and Paragraphs

In order to write a descriptive essay, students must be able to first write descriptive words, descriptive sentences, and descriptive paragraphs. A descriptive essay can be a narrative, a personal recount, a report, or an explanation. The more description and detail that is added to a piece of writing, the more the reader will enjoy and understand the content.

Descriptive Words and Sentences

The key to writing descriptive words is to use a combination of adjectives, adverbs, and sensory words. Students should consider using colorful adjectives and adverbs when describing objects and actions.
For example, the sentence

'the *enormous and furious wave crashed down on the rocks with a thundering blast,*'

includes several adjectives and adverbs that describe the wave. This effect can also be used by younger students.

For example, "*the big wave crashed on the sharp rocks,*" is still more descriptive than just saying that "the wave hit the rocks".

Students should also incorporate 'sensory' words when writing. Sensory words are words that show the effects of the five senses. Students should combine sensory words to create sentences. For example, instead of just saying, "*I sat on the beach and heard the birds as they flew in the air,*" we can say, "*I felt the soft sand under my feet as I gazed at the seagulls gliding over the ocean*".

Descriptive Paragraphs

A descriptive paragraph should have a topic sentence and supporting sentences that contain descriptive words. The paragraph should be organized in time-order sequence. It should also include adjectives, adverbs, and sensory words. The last sentence in the paragraph should conclude or summarize the entire paragraph and link back to the topic sentence.

Descriptive Writing – Paragraphs
Grades 4-6

A **descriptive paragraph** tells about a topic. The paragraph should include several sentences that clearly describe the topic. The paragraph should include sensory details that cater to all the senses: sight, smell, touch, hearing, smelling, and tasting.

You must begin your descriptive paragraph with a **topic sentence**. The topic sentence should tell the reader what the paragraph is about and it should grab the reader's attention (could be a question, surprising statement…).

Example:

1. Begin with a topic: My Room
2. Write some dot jot sensory words.
3. Write a topic sentence and paragraph.

The sights: - my bed - my desk, chair and computer -pictures of cars on wall -shirt on the floor - poster of hockey teams - night table with lamp -bed is not made -closet -dresser -alarm clock
The tastes: -there are not tastes
The smells: -smelly socks in my closet -fresh shirts in my dresser drawer
The textures: -soft bed spread -smooth carpet -firm chair
The sounds: -computer start up -creaking bed -squeaky chair

Topic sentence: **Do you like your room? Well I love mine!**

This makes the reader want to read on because they wonder why the author loves their room.

Paragraph:

Do you like your room? Well I love mine!

The first thing I see is my comfy bed with my soft bed spread. My bed is great even though it creaks when I lie down in it. Beside my bed are my desk, chair, and computer. It's a great place to do homework! I easily sit in my firm chair, dig my feet in the smooth carpet, listen for my computer to start up, and start to work. I have posters of my favorite hockey teams right above my computer. I also have colorful posters of race cars all over my room. This morning, my mom put my laundry away in my dresser. When I opened my shirt drawer, a strong fresh smell caught my attention. I love my room! My mom sometimes complains of the smell from my socks in the closet, but it doesn't bother me because my room is the best place!

Go to the next page…

Think about a playground near where you live in order to write a descriptive paragraph.

1. Fill in the chart.
2. Write a topic sentence. (e.g. My Park)
3. Write a descriptive paragraph.

The sights:
The tastes:
The smells:
The textures:
The sounds:

Essay Writing

You can write directly on this page, photocopy this page, or write on a separate piece of paper.

Title: ______________________________

Topic Sentence:

____

Paragraph:

____

____

____

____

____

____

____

____

____

____

Answers will vary

Descriptive Personal Narratives/Essays

When writing a personal narrative, it is important for students to remember to pay attention to descriptive words and personal feelings.

Students can improve their personal narratives by incorporating the following ideas:

Use the 5 Senses

The 5 senses (hearing, tasting, touching, smelling, seeing) bring a piece of writing to life. Students should remember to use descriptive adjectives and verbs that enhance the five senses. For example, instead of writing, "the girl smelled the flower", students can write, "the sweet scent of freshness from the flower glided into her nose".

Add Some Dialogue

Dialogue often gives a narrative a sense of 'life' as well. When applicable, students should try to incorporate some dialogue in order to give the writing a 'human feel'. Keep in mind, some narratives might be better off without dialogue. Students should consider whether or not a conversation (i.e. dialogue) fits in with the content.

Use Thoughts and Emotions

It is extremely important for writers to add their personal thoughts and emotions in their writing. This gives writing that 'personal' feel to it. When writing a narrative, students should try to write about a topic that they are somewhat emotional about (when I refer to 'emotional' I am referring to both positive and negative emotions). When writers feel strongly about something, whether it is positive or negative, those emotions will come out in their writing.

Descriptive Writing – Essays Grades 4-8

A **descriptive essay** is a piece of writing that includes specific language, sensory details, and detail.

A descriptive essay is organized like a paragraph. It has a **beginning**, **middle**, and a **conclusion**.

Steps Required to Write an Organized Descriptive Essay:

1. The beginning or introductory paragraph tells who or what your essay is about. Your topic sentence should 'grab' the reader's attention (See the lesson on topic sentences). Introduce 3 major ideas about your topic. A good topic sentence grabs the reader's attention with a surprising statement or a question.

2. The next 3 paragraphs describe and provide detail about the topic introduced in the first paragraph (See the lesson on paragraph writing). Each paragraph should have a topic sentence. Make sure that your 3 topics are interesting. Do your research before you decide on your 3 topics so that you will be able to find the information you are looking for.

3. The final paragraph concludes or sums up the topic. Make sure you have a strong ending.

Next page…

Let's assume you are writing a descriptive essay about your favorite superhero. This is what your outline should look like.

Title	**Superman**
Topic Sentence and Introductory Paragraph	**Do you know anyone who wears the letter's' on his chest? Did you know that the man of steel is the most recognized superhero in the world?** (After the topic sentence, I will write my 3 topics)
1st Paragraph Topic Sentence	(This paragraph will discuss how, when, and where the idea of Superman was created) **Superman was officially born in 1932.**
2nd Paragraph Topic Sentence	(This paragraph will discuss Superman's character, powers, and abilities) **Superman stands for truth and justice and he possesses extraordinary powers.**
3rd Paragraph Topic Sentence	(This paragraph will discuss the impact that Superman has on culture) **Superman's character has led to the creation of many other superheroes and has contributed to the merchandising of numerous products, movies, and cartoons.**
Conclusion	(A strong sentence should sum up the 3 topics) **Superman has had an enormous impact on children of all ages throughout the world.**

Next page…

Essay Writing

You can use the following chart (directly or photocopy it) in order to organize a descriptive essay (use point form notes). When the chart is completed, write a rough draft and edit it thoroughly.

Title	
Topic Sentence and Introductory Paragraph (Introduce the 3 topics)	
1st Paragraph Topic Sentence	
2nd Paragraph Topic Sentence	
3rd Paragraph Topic Sentence	
Conclusion (A strong sentence should sum up the 3 topics)	

Editing and Revising

Editing and Proofreading Checklist

Have your child use the following checklist when he or she is editing a piece of writing. I suggest that your child use a different color for each editing type (e.g. punctuation in green, capitals in blue, etc…).

I checked for:

Punctuation
___ . periods at the end of sentences
___ ? question marks at the end of questions
___ ! exclamation marks to show expression
___ "" quotation marks around speaking parts
___ , commas are used properly
___ ' apostrophes are used correctly

Capitals
___ at the beginning of each sentence
___ in proper names and dates
___ for the word 'I'
___ my title has capital letters

Spelling
A good idea!
___ spellchecker or dictionary
___ I checked words with 5 or more letters

Sentences
___ good word choice
___ missing words/extra words
___ no fragments or run-ons
___ I properly indented the first sentence of a paragraph

Revising

It is important for students to learn how to correctly revise their work before handing it in. Revision includes correcting grammar, spelling, and content.

You can easily help your child learn to revise his or her writing.

Organization
Make sure that the topic sentences and paragraphs are organized accordingly. If the topic sentence or introduction contains, ideas a, b, and c, then the paragraphs should be organized in the same order (i.e. a, b, and c). Perhaps some paragraphs have to be re-ordered if they are not organized accordingly.

Ideas
Go over the main ideas that are presented. Make sure that all the important points are expressed. If the writing is an opinion or persuasive, make sure that both sides of the argument are presented.

Strengths
Start off by underlining or putting a note beside the sentences or paragraphs that demonstrate good writing. This will make the rest of the revision less painful.

Weaknesses
Focus on one aspect of revision at a time. For example, start off looking for missing details, then work on grammar, and then focus on sentence structure etc...

Read Out Loud
By far, the best way to revise writing is to read it out loud. This is the best method to catch mistakes than weren't caught when reading silently.

Information

Should more information be added? Make sure the topic sentences state the main idea and make sure that the rest of the paragraph contains the supporting details. Also, make sure that the concluding statement supports the topic sentence. Are facts or data required? Don't be shy to delete or cross out any irrelevant information and make sure that there isn't too much repetition.

Show, Don't Tell

Use the 5 senses to add description to a piece of writing. Try not to use a 'passive' voice. Instead, use an 'active' voice. Verbs are good words to use because they add more 'movement' to a piece of writing.

Detail, Detail, Detail

Check for detail, especially when writing a narrative. Make sure that the reader definitely knows exactly what is being referred to when they read such words as 'they', 'him', 'it', etc...

Students should use a word processing program when revising. This will make the entire process much easier because students can move paragraphs, delete sentence, and add in words or ideas.

Explanation Writing – Essays
Grades 2-3

An **explanation** is a reason for something. When writing an explanation, you must add details and use descriptive writing.

Read the following example of an explanation for being late for school.

> I was late for school because of my little brother and baby sister.
>
> My little brother, James, didn't want to get out of bed. Then he started to cry when my mother decided to give him warm oatmeal instead of toast for breakfast. My baby sister, Sarah, cried all morning long. First, my mom had to change her stinky diaper and then, my mom had to clean up the mess that my sister made in the kitchen. Sarah threw her bowl of raspberry applesauce all over the kitchen floor. I was very frustrated because I wanted to get to school on time.
>
> I was late for school because my mom had to deal with my brother and sister and she couldn't get me to school on time.

How I wrote a good explanation.

1. The first sentence tells why I was late.
2. I added details to the reasons why I was late. I mentioned my brother and sister's names, the foods my brother didn't want, and my sister's mess.
3. I added descriptive words such as: 'warm oatmeal', 'stinky diaper', and 'raspberry applesauce'.
4. I used expressive language such as 'I was frustrated' to show how I felt.

Next page…

This chart will help organize your next explanation writing assignment.

Write a good first sentence to introduce your explanation.
Go back to your explanation and add details to your writing. Write the details here.
Go back to your explanation and add descriptive words. Write the words here.
Go back to your explanation and write what you saw, felt, heard, or tasted. Add the descriptive language here.

Now, rewrite your explanation and use the information and words from the chart to fill in the details and descriptions.

Explanation Writing – Essays Grades 4-6

An **explanation** is writing that tries to explain how things come to be or the way they are.

Read the following example of an explanation for the digestive system.

How the Digestive System Works

The digestive system is made up of the digestive tract which is a series of organs joined in a long, twisting tube that help the body break down and absorb food.

The digestive system consists of the mouth, esophagus, stomach, small and large intestine, gall bladder, liver, and pancreas.

First, the saliva chemically breaks down the food and the teeth grind it up so that it can pass down the esophagus. The esophagus is about 10 inches (25 cm) long and it moves food from the back of your throat to your stomach. The J- shaped stomach then breaks down the food into a liquid mixture, and then dumps it into the small intestine. After the stomach empties the food and juice mixture into the small intestine, the juices of two other digestive organs mix with the food. One of these organs, the pancreas, produces a juice that contains many enzymes that break down the carbohydrate, fat, and protein in food. The small intestine is about 2 inches (5 cm) around and 22 feet (7 m) long. It breaks down the food even more so that the body can absorb vitamins, minerals, proteins, fats, and carbohydrates. The liver and gallbladder help the intestine to digest and absorb the food. Food can spend up to 4 hours in your intestine.

The digestive system is a very important system of the body. Without it, we couldn't get the nutrients we need to grow properly and stay healthy.

Continued on next page…

Elements of an Organized and Well Written Explanation

1. The 1st paragraph stated **what the explanation was about.**

2. The second paragraph described the **parts** involved.

3. The 3rd paragraph (the body) explained **'how it worked'** and the 'cause and effect'.

4. The last paragraph concluded the explanation and **explained its importance.**

On the next page you will find a template to help you organize an explanation. You can write in the chart or photocopy it for repeated use. Use point form notes in the chart then write a rough copy.

Essay Writing

Topic	
Definition What is it?	
Parts Describe the Parts	
How it Works Cause and Effect	
Conclusion/ Importance	
Facts/ Special Information	

Gathering Ideas for Writing

So now we know what we want to write our report on. We have worked hard to come up with an idea. Now what?

There are some obvious and not so obvious sources to gather information.

Obvious Sources (good for informational essays, expositions, and reports)

- Go online. Find reliable sources of information. Get information from several websites and make sure you reference your sources. An online encyclopedia is a great place to start.
- Read books and magazines. Again, make sure you cite your sources. Make sure you don't copy word for word. Write some point form notes then put them into your own words.
- Interview people in the community. Who better to talk to than a doctor if you are doing a report on the digestive system?
- Visit the museum or local science center. These places are perfect for finding reliable information.

Not So Obvious Sources (good for stories, narratives, and essays)

- Talk to friends, teachers, and family members. Get some good ideas from others.
- For narratives and stories, go people watching. Examine people's mannerisms when you are at the mall.
- A great way to get ideas for characters is to watch television and movies. Choose some characters you like and create your own character with similar traits.

Try to use as many sources as you can and you will find that you will have a great deal of information on any topic.

Generating Essay Ideas

Students often find it difficult to develop writing ideas. Unless students are given a specific topic with specific sub-topics, students can spend a great deal of time deciding what to write about.

Good writing ideas come from many sources. It requires more than just sitting around thinking of an idea or surfing the internet. There are several ways to generate good ideas for writing.

Regardless of whether it is an essay, an informative report, or science report, good ideas will make all writing assignments stand out above the rest.

Here are some ways that you can generate good writing ideas:

- **Reflect upon personal experiences**. Have you been to specific places? Have you seen interesting things? Use your personal background knowledge and experiences in order to come up with ideas. For example, assume you have to write a report on a specific cultural aspect of a country. Which country? What cultural aspect? Perhaps your grandparents come from England and you enjoy soccer. There's an idea! You can write a report on the cultural impact of soccer on the English economy (for example). The point here is for you to find something that you can relate to. This will help you generate ideas and it might make the project more interesting.

- **Read stories, books, and magazines on a topic you are interested in.** By reading books and stories about personally interesting topics, you can get more ideas and gain different perspectives. For example, assume you like computers. You already have a good knowledge of home computers. Let's say you read a magazine story about a new kind of home computer or a new application or program. Having read the article on a topic that interests you, you've just stumbled upon a new idea for a report or essay.

- **Talk to friends and family.** Sometimes friends and family know you better than you know yourself. Assume you have no idea what to write about. Your parent or friend can remind you about something you did, somewhere you went, or some interest you have had in the past that you forgot about. Or, they might simply come up with a great idea for you. Don't be shy, ask others.

- **Go Online.** It's unbelievable how visiting one site about a topic can lead you somewhere completely different. You can get on the internet, have a specific topic in mind, and within a few minutes, find yourself reading about an interesting topic that has nothing to do with the first web-site you visited.

- **Create a topic web.** Let's say you are interested in cars, for example. Write the word 'car' in the middle of a blank page and circle it. Draw lines from the circle with 'cars' in it to create other words and put them in circles. The other words must have something to do with cars. For example, you may have written down the word 'Ferrari', or 'engine'. Then, from the words 'Ferrari' and 'engine', draw lines to other related words until you create a word web. By the time you get to the edge of the paper, you may have such words as 'Indy 500', or 'Solar Powered Cars'. This is a great way to generate ideas from your areas of interest.

Having good writing ideas will help your child create informative and interesting pieces of writing. Try as many methods above as you can in order to generate a good writing idea.

Letter Writing

Letter Writing

In the primary grades (1-3) students are introduced to writing a friendly letter.

You can help your child write a friendly letter by focusing on prewriting, writing, and editing techniques.

1. **Prewriting** - Your child should choose a recipient (unless they are already given one by their teacher). He/she should choose someone they feel comfortable with so that he or she will not feel shy and write more freely. Have your child gather all the ideas required for a letter.

Your child can write about the following:

- describe a personal event or accomplishment
- tell about a recent book, movie, or magazine
- share a story of a situation
- ask questions to find out how the recipient is doing

2. **Writing** - Your child should begin by writing a paragraph for each idea on their list. If your child is only writing about one idea, he/she should break down the idea into sub-topics. For example, let's say your child wants to write about a certain event that happened on the weekend. Your child can write about the events leading up to the situation, the situation itself, and what happened after the situation.

3. **Editing** - Your child should check for punctuation, spelling, capitalization, and overall format of the letter. Have your child check over each of these separately. That is, don't have your child start reading and look for spelling, punctuation, and capitalization at the same time. This is overwhelming! Start off with spelling, for example, and then edit the others.

Writing a Friendly Letter
Grades 1-3

A friendly letter has 5 parts:

1. Date
2. Greeting
3. Body
4. Closing
5. Signature.

A comma is needed after the greeting and closing.

Example:

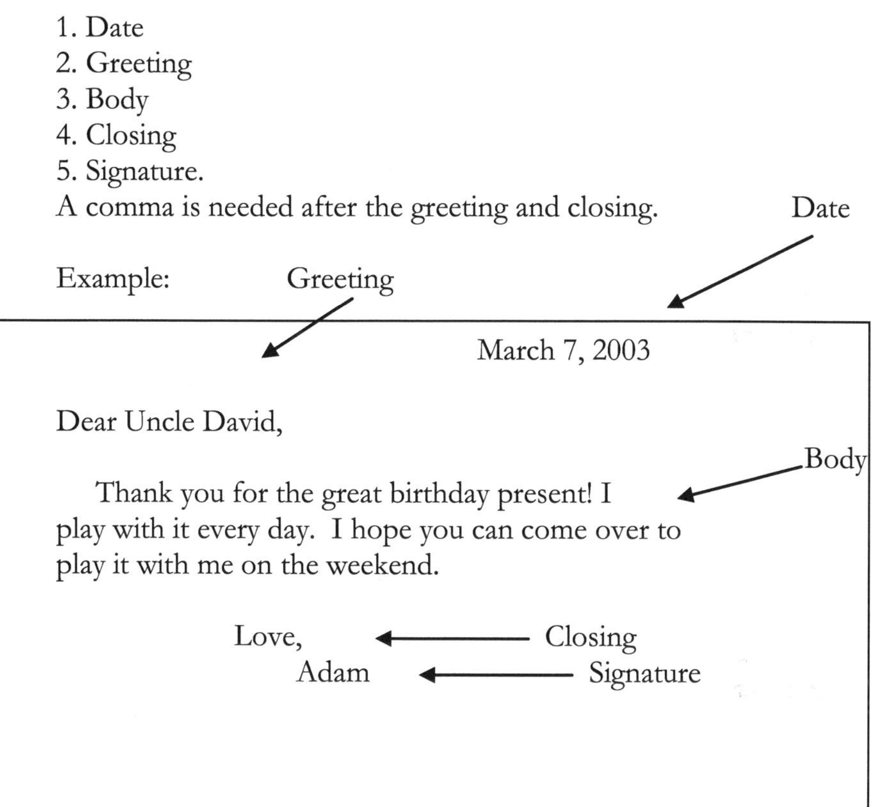

March 7, 2003

Dear Uncle David,

Thank you for the great birthday present! I play with it every day. I hope you can come over to play it with me on the weekend.

Love,
Adam

Next page...

1. Fill in the missing parts of the friendly letter.

2. Label the parts.

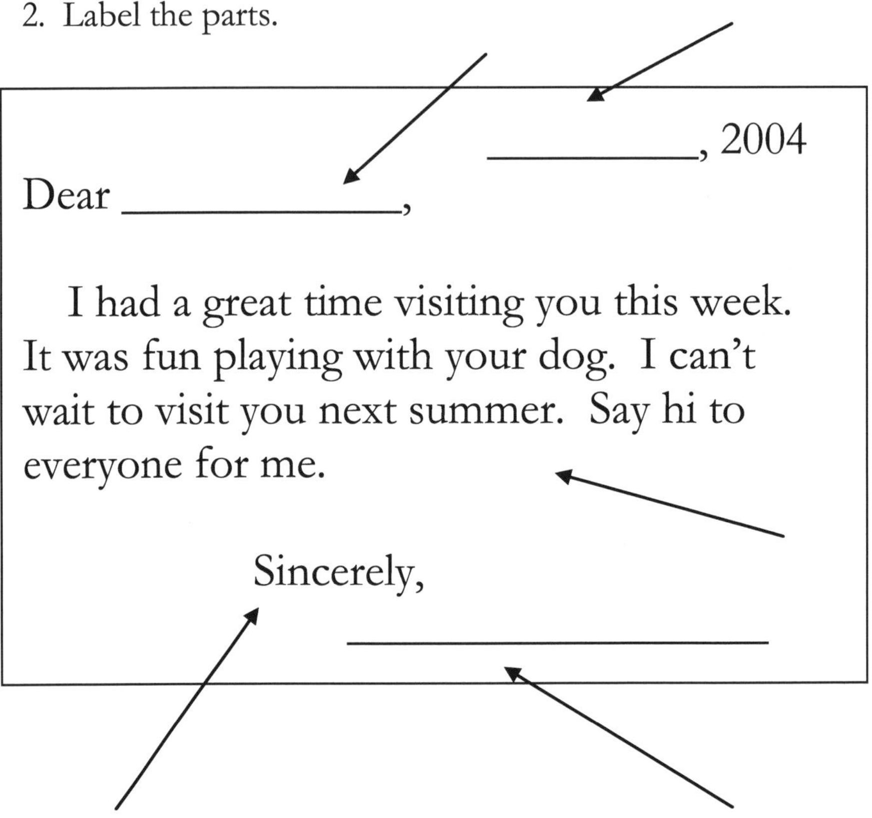

Go to the next page to see some possible answers…

Primary English: Writing Lesson: Friendly Letters

May 10, 2004

Dear Grandma,

I had a great time visiting you this week. It was fun playing with your dog. I can't wait to visit you next summer. Say hi to everyone for me.

Sincerely,

Michael

Date

Greeting

Body

Closing

Signature

These are some possible answers. Make sure that the letter is correctly labeled and the greeting and signature are appropriate.

Business Letters -How to Write a Business Letter

When writing a business letter, students should realize that it is similar to writing a friendly letter. Students should consider who their audience is, what their reason is for writing the letter, and what exactly they want to say.

A business letter does differ from a friendly letter. Students should note the following differences when writing a business letter as opposed to a friendly letter.

- The greeting has a colon (:) in a business letter as opposed to a comma in a friendly letter.

- Business letters contain the writer's address and an 'inside address' which is the address of the person to whom the letter is being written.

- The closing of the business letter is not as casual as a friendly letter. In a friendly letter, we usually write "Love', or "Your Friend". In a business letter, the closing is more formal. We usually write, "Sincerely" or "Yours Truly".

- In a business letter, we put in two signatures. First, we place a handwritten signature and then a typed signature.

Business Letters
Grades 4-6

A business letter is similar to a friendly letter.
A business letter has:
- an **inside address** which is the address of the person to whom you are writing, and **your address at the top right.**
- the **greeting has a colon (:)** after the greeting instead of a comma (,)
- **a body** (this is what you are saying in your letter)
- a **formal closing (e.g. Sincerely, Yours Truly**) instead of a friendly closing such as 'love'
-a **signature** that is **both typed and handwritten**

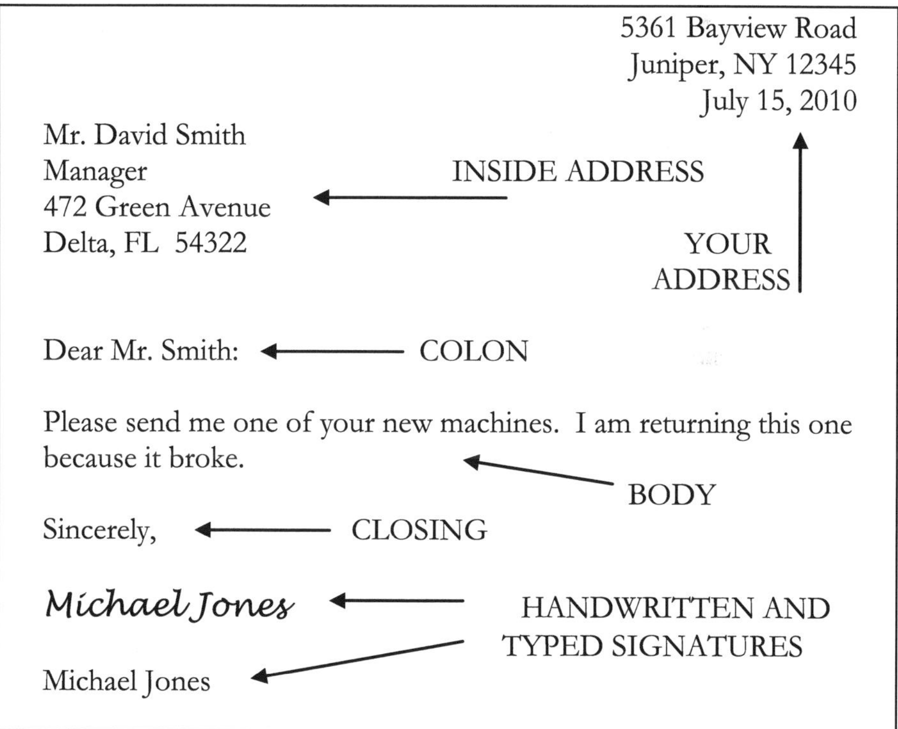
5361 Bayview Road
Juniper, NY 12345
July 15, 2010

Mr. David Smith
Manager
472 Green Avenue
Delta, FL 54322

Dear Mr. Smith:

Please send me one of your new machines. I am returning this one because it broke.

Sincerely,

Michael Jones

Michael Jones

Put the following parts of a business letter in the appropriate position.

Yours Truly,

Dear Mr. Davis:

Kyle MacDonald

Mr. Adam Davis
Editor
25362
496 Apple Street.
Queenstown, VA 48454

Kyle MacDonald

49 River Rd.
Grandview, TX

May 26, 2009

Thank you for reading my article. I hope that you will publish it soon. I am looking forward to speaking with you.

The correct format is on the next page…

Junior English: Writing   Lesson: Writing a Business Letter

49 River Rd.
Grandview, TX 25362
May 26, 2009

Mr. Adam Davis
Editor
496 Apple Street.
Queenstown, VA
48454

Dear Mr. Davis:

Thank you for reading my article. I hope that you will publish it soon. I am looking forward to speaking with you.

Yours Truly,

Kyle MacDonald

Kyle MacDonald

Paragraph Writing

How to Write a Paragraph

It is important that your child organize all writing assignments in school and at home. Writing assignments should be organized according to their specific audience. Procedures, reports, and personal recounts all have different formats. You can help your child to organize his or her writing.

1. Make sure your child knows how to create a topic sentence that introduces the topic. Topic sentences can introduce a paragraph and an entire assignment.

2. Make sure your child understands the basic structure of a paragraph. Since a group of paragraphs make an entire writing assignment, it is important that your child understands the parts that make up the whole.

3. Help your child create 'ideas' about a topic and show your child how to organize those 'ideas' in logical order.

4. Have your child practice writing a procedure. Procedure writing is a great tool to teach students written organization because they require a logical and chronological format.

5. Provide your child with graphic organizers (such as flow charts and brainstorming webs) that allow your child to 'see' the topics on paper. Once your child 'sees' the topics, he or she can start to organize them.

6. Use a word processing program such as Microsoft Office. Your child will be able to separate paragraphs and move them around at will (as opposed to writing the work on paper). This will give your child more flexibility to practice organizing and reorganizing his/her writing.

Types of Paragraphs

All paragraphs have (or should have) a topic sentence that introduces the main idea. The body of the paragraph provides supporting details for the main idea. Finally, a good paragraph should have a closing sentence (unless the paragraph is a narrative which doesn't necessarily give factual information).

There are 4 types of paragraphs:

1. A **descriptive** paragraph describes something.
2. A **narrative** paragraph tells a story.
3. A **persuasive** paragraph discusses an opinion.
4. An **expository** or **explanatory** paragraph explains something.

Descriptive Paragraphs
A descriptive paragraph describes a person, place, thing, or idea. When writing a descriptive paragraph, students should remember to use words that describe the 5 senses (seeing, hearing, tasting, touching, and smelling). Students should remember to tell the reader about the colors, sizes, smells, tastes, and shape things are. It is the writer's objective to make the reader visualize what is being read.

Narrative Paragraph
In a narrative paragraph, students tell a story by sharing and describing experiences. Narrative paragraphs (hence narrative stories) should keep the reader involved and engaged by making the reader want to continue reading. When writing a narrative paragraph, students should include colorful adjectives and descriptive verbs.

Persuasive Paragraph
A persuasive paragraph involves the writer expressing his or her opinion on a topic. The writer wants to convince the reader that his or her point of view is correct and right. Persuasive paragraphs should contain facts and data which support the writer's position.

The writer should support his or her point of view the best that he or she can in order to persuade or convince the reader.

Expository/Explanatory Paragraph

The reason for an expository or explanatory paragraph is to give information about a subject. These paragraphs should explain ideas, give directions, or show a process of how to accomplish something. Expository or explanatory paragraphs should have factual information provided in sequential order. The use of transition words is important when writing an exposition.

Although these paragraphs differ in some ways, they still share some common elements. They should all have a sentence that shows the main idea and other sentences that support the main idea.

Introduction to Paragraphs
Grades 1-3

A paragraph is a group of sentences about the same topic.

A good paragraph has the following:

1. The first line is indented (move 5 spaces before typing).
2. The first sentence is the topic sentence which has the main idea.
3. Each other sentence supports and tells about the main idea.

Example:

The first line is indented. **The first sentence is the topic sentence (main idea).**

I enjoy the summer break. The summer is fun. Last year, I went to camp for two weeks. I had a great time. This summer, I will play with my friends and go to the park. The park is a lot of fun. During the summer break I also visit my grandparents and we always have a good time.

The other sentences support the main idea that, "I enjoy the summer break,"

Read the following paragraph and answer the questions.

Math is my best subject! Last term, I had an A+ in math. It was my highest mark on my report card. I am good at adding and subtracting. I practice my math every night so that I can do well in math class. My teacher is very proud of me because I always put up my hand to answer questions in math class.

1. Put a check mark where the first line is indented.
2. Circle the topic sentence.
3. Underline two sentences that support the main idea.

The answers are on the next page…

Primary English: Writing Lesson: Introduction to Paragraphs

✓ Math is my best subject! Last term, I had an A+ in math. It was my highest mark on my report card. I am good at adding and subtracting. I practice my math every night so that I can do well in math class. My teacher is very proud of me because I always put up my hand to answer questions in math class.

Paragraph Format
Grades 1-3

A **paragraph** is a group of sentences about one main idea. When writing a paragraph, remember to do the following:

1. **Indent** the first line.
2. **Capitalize** the first word of each sentence.
3. **Punctuate** each sentence.

Correct the following paragraph by following the three rules.

the sun gives light to the earth, it makes our weather change from season to season, Sometimes it is sunny and warm and other times it is cloudy and cold, the sun's rays are strong during the summer and weak during the winter,

After corrections.

The sun gives light to the earth. It makes our weather change from season to season. Sometimes it is sunny and warm and other times it is cloudy and cold. The sun's rays are strong during the summer and weak during the winter.

Correct the next paragraph by following the three rules.

my family is going to Niagara Falls, tomorrow we plan to get there early, my mom will take my brother to the haunted house first, my dad and I will go see the falls and then have some dinner, we will sleep in the hotel and then go for breakfast in the morning,

Use the lines on the next page…

____

____

____

____

____

____

____

____

____

____

____

____

____

See the correct answer on the next page…

Primary English: Writing Lesson: Paragraph Format

My family is going to Niagara Falls. Tomorrow we plan to get there early. My mom will take my brother to the haunted house first. My dad and I will go see the falls and then have some dinner. We will sleep in the hotel and then go for breakfast in the morning.

Planning a Paragraph

It is important to plan a paragraph because a combination of good paragraphs is the backbone for a good piece of writing.

Make a Plan

Before writing a paragraph, it is important to determine the bigger picture.

1. First determine what the topic of the paragraph will be. The rest of the paragraph will support the topic sentence.

2. Who is the audience? Will a teacher or other students be reading the paragraph? The paragraph should be consistent with the rest of the writing. It should be more complex for adult readers and simpler for younger readers.

3. What is the form? Determine what type of paragraph it will be (i.e. factual, narrative?).

Get the Information

It is time to gather all the details for the paragraph. The topic sentence must introduce the idea of the paragraph and the supporting sentence must support the topic.

<u>Descriptive paragraphs</u> - should have details that focus on the five senses (i.e. focus on adjectives and descriptive words)

<u>Narrative paragraphs</u> - should contain details about an experience and problems in sequential order

<u>Persuasive paragraphs</u> - must contain facts, figures and proof to back up your opinion

<u>Expository paragraphs</u> - have facts to explain a process or

phenomenon

Organize

Make sure the topic sentence of the paragraph is first. Next, make sure the supporting sentences give proof, facts, or information that supports the topic sentence. The last sentence is the closing sentence. This sentence sums up the paragraph.

Editing

Read your paragraph out loud. Make sure you have a good introduction, supporting details, and your conclusion. Check spelling, punctuation, and sentence structure.

Remember, good paragraphs lead to good reports and essays.

Writing an Informational Paragraph Grades 4-6

An **informational paragraph** is a paragraph that gives facts. Informational paragraphs can be found in reports and essays.
e.g.

Alexander Graham Bell

Alexander Graham Bell invented the telephone. He was born in Scotland in 1847. He moved to Canada and then on to Boston. In 1872, Bell founded his own school for deaf-mutes and shortly thereafter, he was appointed Professor of Vocal Physiology at Boston University. Bell needed an assistant to help with his idea and he found a man named Thomas Watson, who was a young electrician and model maker. The two labored on a project for almost a year until a happy accident occurred on June 2, 1875. While Watson worked to loosen a reed that was wound around an electromagnet, Bell heard a familiar 'twang' sound. He then realized this sound could be recreated with the human voice. The telephone had been invented! After patenting the invention and staging a demonstration of the telephone at the Centennial Exhibition in Philadelphia in 1876, Bell went on to form the Bell Telephone Company in 1877.

1. Why is the topic (1st) sentence important? It is important because it tells us what the paragraph is going to be about.
2. What is the main idea? The main idea is that he invented the telephone.
3. What are some of the facts?

a) He was born in Scotland in 1847.
b) In 1872, Bell founded his own school for deaf-mutes..
c) ...on June 2, 1875... The telephone had been invented
d) Bell went on to form the Bell Telephone Company in 1877.

4. What is the conclusion? Bell went on to form the Bell Telephone Company in 1877.

The next time you are going to write an essay or report you can use the following chart to help organize your paragraphs.

Topic	
Main Idea	
Topic Sentence	
Details	
Conclusion	

Personal Narratives and Recounts

Personal Narratives

A personal narrative, or recount, is a true story about something that happened to the person who is writing, hence, it is personal writing.

The following description will help you help your child write a personal piece of writing.

A personal writing piece is the retelling or recounting of someone's past experiences. They are usually told in the first person "I". Personal writing is descriptive accounts with details that support the writer's perspective. It is also important to know that personal writing is structured in a chronological order. The focus of the personal writing piece is to create sequential events that involve the author. There are several types of personal writing such as, personal recounts, autobiographies, letters, diaries, eye-witness accounts, and journals.

Personally written narratives usually begin with an opening statement that introduces the 5w's (who, what, where, when, why). The important events are discussed in detail throughout the body in paragraphs. Each paragraph should discuss a particular event. The beginning of each paragraph should start with a linking word such as: first, after, soon, when, later, or finally. The last part of the personal narrative should include a concluding statement. This concluding statement should sum up the author's summary of the events.

The personal writing piece should also have the proper language conventions. The participants in the recount should be as specific as possible (e.g. instead of my aunt, it should be my Aunt Jenny). Recounts should also be written in past tense. Students should edit their work by paying attention to their verb tenses. Linking words that clearly illustrate the chronology should be used. Details and a first person perspective are also essential for a well written personal narrative.

Gathering Ideas for a Personal Narrative

Personal narratives require some sense of introspection and reflection. You must be able to take a step back and look at your life. You should consider the following when gathering ideas for a personal narrative:

Hobbies and Interests
What are some of your hobbies or interests? Do prefer a certain sport? Perhaps you are interested in science, animals, or video games. What do you like to read about or watch on television? Is music important to you? By focusing in on an interest, you will be able to narrow down a topic. Then, when you have a topic (e.g. dogs) you can then write about your experiences with that topic.

Places You Have Visited
Where have you been? You can write a great deal about your time in the dentist's office or at the zoo. Maybe you were on a cruise or went camping in the forest. Reflect back on the activities you did, the feelings you had, and the experiences you can remember from these places.

Who Do You Spend Time With?
Think about the people who you spend time with. Who has the greatest impact on your life? Include friends, family, and role models. Reflect back to the good, bad, and special times you have had with these people. Do you immediately think about the every day events or special events with the people who are close to you?

You should take some time to write down some notes for each of the above headings. Then, you can combine their notes to write a personal narrative. For example, you can write a personal narrative about a recent family vacation to a cottage. You can include the specific place, the activities, and people who made the trip to the cottage memorable. They key here is for you to categorize your experiences, and then put them together to write a descriptive personal narrative.

Personal Narratives/Recount Writing
Grades 1-3

A personal narrative, or recount, is a retelling of your own experiences.
You are the writer and you discuss something that happened to you.
A recount is written in past tense and is always written from first person "I".

Here is an example of a recount.

Title

My Day at the Park

Setting

Yesterday my family and I went to the park.

When we got there, we took out our sports equipme[illegible] played. I first played soccer and then catch.

After playing, I decided to relax under a tree. I was tired so I asked my family to play cards.

An hour later, we decided to get our picnic lunch ready. My mom took out the basket and blanket.

During lunch, a cute squirrel came right up to our blanket. I gave the squirrel a piece of bread. The squirrel ran away.

When I returned home I read my book and watched television. I had a great time at the park.

Important:

1. Notice the underlined 'linking' words that show that the events are in order of time.
2. Notice how each event is in its own paragraph.
3. Notice the conclusion, "I had a great time at the park."

Go to the next page…

Put the following parts of a recount in order in the chart below.

After we saw the African animals, I told my mom that I was hungry so she gave me some lunch. I had my favorite, pizza!

I had a great time at the zoo! I can't wait to go again.

A Day at the Zoo

I went to the zoo last weekend with my family.

When we got to the zoo, I asked my parents to go and see the elephants. The elephants are in the African animal exhibit.

Before lunch, I went on a camel ride. It was really bumpy. I almost fell off!

Title
Setting
Event 1
Event 2
Event 3
Conclusion

Primary English: Writing   Lesson: Personal Narrative / Recount

Title	A Day at the Zoo
Setting	I went to the zoo last weekend with my family.
Event 1	When we got to the zoo, I asked my parents to go and see the elephants. The elephants are in the African animal exhibit.
Event 2	After we saw the African animals, I told my mom that I was hungry so she gave me some lunch. I had my favorite, pizza!
Event 3	After lunch, I went on a camel ride. It was really bumpy. I almost fell off!
Conclusion	I had a great time at the zoo! I can't wait to go again.

Now, write your personal narrative/recount in essay format (that is, write it with a title and paragraphs.

See the next page…

A Day at the Zoo

I went to the zoo last weekend with my family.

When we got to the zoo, I asked my parents to go and see the elephants. The elephants are in the African animal exhibit.

After we saw the African animals, I told my mom that I was hungry so she gave me some lunch. I had my favorite, pizza!

After lunch, I went on a camel ride. It was really bumpy. I almost fell off!

I had a great time at the zoo! I can't wait to go again.

Personal Narratives/Recount Writing Grades 4-6

A **personal narrative or recount** is a retelling of something that happened to the person who tells it. Personal narratives are based on the experiences of the writer. A recount can be in the form of autobiographies, diaries, journals, or letters.

Personal Narratives have the following:
1. They are told in the first person, "I".
2. They are very detailed and descriptive.
3. They use realistic language to support the author's experiences.
4. They are usually told in a chronological order.

Read the personal narrative/recount and answer the questions.

My Best Day

by David

Last Friday was my best day ever! It was even better than my last birthday! I had a great time with my family.

First, at about 3:00, we went to play mini-golf. The course was awesome! It had a sunken ship, a tall white lighthouse, and a pond with real fish! I had a good game. I beat my mom and my sister by my dad beat all of us. He's really good!

After mini-golf, we went to the Burger Palace for dinner. It's my favorite place. I had a Monster Burger with cheese and French fries with gravy. My mom couldn't believe I ate the whole thing! I was surprised when my dad let us have ice cream for dessert because he usually makes sure we eat healthy. Maybe he was happy because he won at mini-golf. Anyhow, I ordered the Frozen Frankenstein. It had 3 scoops of ice cream with gummy worms, whipped cream, and chocolate sauce. My mom couldn't believe I finished it.

Shortly after we finished dessert, we went to see the new Disney movie. It was really funny. My sister and I laughed the entire time.

In the end, I had a great day at mini-golf, the Burger Palace, and the movie. This was the best day ever!

Questions.

1. How did the writer get your attention right at the beginning?

____

____

2. List the details that the writer used to show his emotions.

____

3. List the transition phrases that showed you that the recount was in chronological order.

____

____

____

____

4. Does the narrative have a concluding statement? What is it?

____

5. What is your proof that this is a personal narrative/recount?

____

____

____

____

Answers are on the next page…

Answers

1. The writer got my attention by saying, "Last Friday was my best day ever! It was even better than my last birthday!"

2.

- It's my favorite place
- I was surprised
- This was the best day ever!
- I ate the whole thing
- I was surprised

3.

1. Last Friday
2. First
3. After mini-golf
4. Shortly after we finished
5. In the end

4. Yes. The concluding statement is, "In the end, I had a great day at mini-golf, the Burger Palace, and the movie. This was the best day ever!

5. It is someone's experience. It is told in the 1st person "I" and it is in chronological order.

On the next page, you will find a graphic organizer to help with future personal narratives and recounts.

Personal Narrative/ Recount

Topic	
Setting **5 W's**	
Event 1	
Event 2	
Event 3	
Event 4	
Concluding Statement	

Persuasive Expositions

Persuasive Expositions

The purpose of persuasive writing (or an exposition) is to create ideas and support them with proof in order to present a logical argument with a point of view.

An exposition must have the following in correct order:

1. An introductory paragraph stating the topic, problem, and point of view.
2. A paragraph that supports the author's point of view.
3. A paragraph that goes against the author's point of view.
4. An evaluation or summary that reiterates the author's point of view.

Some examples of persuasive writing are:
Do video games promote violence in young people?
Should schools have vending machines?
All animals should be micro chipped.

Expositions (persuasive writing) should persuade readers to agree with a writer's particular point of view. It must compare or contrast issues that will persuade the reader that the author's point of view is correct. Finally, the writing should present all points in order to form a logical conclusion based on the information and proof given by the writer.

Students must make sure that they:

- Start their opinion clearly.
- Gave strong reasons to support their opinion.
- Organized their reasons in logical order.
- Presented both sides of the argument.
- Clearly indicate what they want the readers to think regarding the issue.

Persuasive/Exposition Writing Grades 4-8

The purpose of persuasive writing (or exposition) is to develop ideas and support them with proof in order to create a logical argument with your point of view.

Example:

Hunting and Freedom of Choice

There has been an ongoing debate as to whether or not hunting should be legal. People who wish to hunt responsibly should be allowed to do so.

Many families, want to be self-reliant and provide for their families. There are many people who have gone to many gun safety classes and are very responsible when hunting. They eat the meat from the animals that they shoot and are considerate of the environment. In this day and age, it's getting harder and harder for rural families to make ends meet so they decide to go hunting in order to put food on the table.

In 2006 in the United States, about 12 million people enjoyed hunting and over 2 billion dollars has been pumped into the American economy from hunting supplies and trips.

It is well known that there are also irresponsible hunters as well. There are several hundred hunting accidents in the United States each year including some deaths. It is apparent that some people are against other people owning guns and killing animals. Some people feel that hunting animals is cruel and violent.

Ultimately, people should have the right to hunt if they are responsible and it means feeding their families. Hunting is excellent for the economy and it is not cruel if people eat the animals they hunt.

Go to next page...

There has been an ongoing debate as to whether or not hunting should be legal. People who wish to hunt responsibly should be allowed to do so.
This paragraph is an overview stating the topic, the problem, and the writer's point of view.

Many families, want to be self-reliant and provide for their families. There are many people who have gone to many gun safety classes and are very responsible when hunting. They eat the meat from the animals that they shoot and are considerate of the environment. In this day and age, it's getting harder and harder for rural families to make ends meet so they decide to go hunting in order to put food on the table.

In 2006 in the United States, about 12 million people enjoyed hunting and over 2 billion dollars has been pumped into the American economy from hunting supplies and trips.
These paragraphs show the arguments FOR the writer's point of view. The writer supports the point of view with evidence.

It is well known that there are also irresponsible hunters as well. There are several hundred hunting accidents in the United States each year including some deaths. It is apparent that some people are against other people owning guns and killing animals. Some people feel that hunting animals is cruel and violent.
This paragraph gives examples for the arguments AGAINST the author's point of view.

Ultimately, people should have the right to hunt if they are responsible and it means feeding their families. Hunting is excellent for the economy and it is not cruel if people eat the animals they hunt.
The last paragraph is the evaluation which reiterates (goes over) the writer's point of view that was mentioned throughout the entire text.

Use the blank chart on the next page for persuasive writing assignments you will do in the future.

Title	
Problem and Point of View	
Arguments FOR	
Arguments AGAINST	
Evaluation/ Reiteration	

Procedures

Procedure Writing

There is actually a procedure to writing procedures!

Writing a procedure is a great way for students to practice organization and detail writing skills. In order to write a procedure, students will learn how to write text that follows a pattern by listing steps that show how to do something.

Procedures are usually associated with writing science experiments. They also include recipes and 'how to' manuals. Students can write a procedure in science, social studies, and math.

You can help your child organize a procedure by following these steps (I guess you can say that this is also a procedure). Each of the following should be in its own paragraph.

1. Your child should list the 'goal or aim' of the procedure. This is an outline of what is to be done.

2. Then, your child should include any materials, instruments, or ingredients needed for the procedure.

3. The method is the most important part of the procedure. The method is a list of steps, either in list form or in paragraphs.

4. The last part of a procedure is the evaluation. The evaluation states whether or not the goal was achieved.

Your child should use linking words that illustrate a chronological order. The procedure should also be written in present tense and towards a general audience.

Procedure Writing
Grades 1-3

The purpose of **writing a procedure** is to give clear, simple to follow directions in the order in which they are to be followed.

In a procedure, you must have the following:
1. A Title.
2. What do you need? (ingredients, utensils)
3. Write down every step in order.
4. Special instructions that are not included in the steps.

Example: Write a procedure for making a pepperoni pizza.

How to Make a Pepperoni Pizza

In order to make a pepperoni pizza, **you need**: dough, cheese, tomato sauce, and pepperoni. You will also need a rolling pin, cheese grater, spoon, oven, and an adult to help with cutting, grating, and cooking.

Step 1: Use the rolling pin to flatten the dough until you get a large thin circle.
Step 2: Take a spoon and spread the tomato sauce all over the dough.
Step 3: Grate the cheese and cut the pepperoni into thin slices.
Step 4: Spread the grated cheese and pepperoni slices over the tomato sauce. Make sure you spread out the cheese and pepperoni.
Step 5: Put the pizza in the oven until the crust gets brown.

Make sure you have an adult help with cutting, grating, and cooking. Never use a knife or oven without adult supervision. When the pizza is done, cut it into slices and enjoy!

Write a procedure to make a ham and cheese sandwich with butter.

How To _______________

In order to make a

____

____

____

Step 1:

____

Step 2:

____

Step 3:

____

Step 4:

____

Step 5:

____

Make sure that

____

____

____

When

____

_

Procedure Writing
Grades 4-6

The purpose of **writing a procedure** is to give clear, simple to follow directions in the order in which they are to be followed.

In a procedure, you must have the following:
1. **Goal or Aim** – What is to be done?
2. **Requirements** – tools, instruments, parts
3. **Steps** –What is to be done? First step to last step.
4. **Evaluation** – Was the goal or aim achieved?

E.g. Write a procedure for replacing batteries in a remote control car.

Replacing Batteries in a Remote Control Car

If your remote control car doesn't work it probably means that the batteries are worn out and must be replaced in the car and/or the remote.

In order to do this installation, you need a screwdriver with various heads and three AA batteries.

The following procedure will illustrate the correct installation of new batteries.

Follow these steps:

1. Undo the screws under the bottom of the car.
2. Take off the back cover.
3. Remove the old batteries and replace them with new ones. Pay attention to the positioning of the batteries (e.g. + and -).
4. Replace the cover and tighten the screws.
5. Turn the switch on and try the car.
6. If the car doesn't work, repeat steps 1-5 with the remote.

If your car didn't work after switching the batteries in the car itself, then it should work after you switched the batteries in the remote.

On the next page, you will find a template for future procedures.

Topic	
Goal or Aim? What is to be done?	
Requirements? -tools -instruments -parts	
Steps -in order	
Evaluation Was the goal or aim achieved?	

Report Writing

Report Writing

A report is a factual piece of writing that contains information. Reports involve research to explore a topic.

The key behind writing a good report is to be well organized. Students must learn to organize their ideas and present them in a clear and succinct.

If your child is writing a report, you can help him/her organize it effectively at home.

1. Have your child choose a specific topic for the report (granted your child has a choice).

2. Your child should decide on 3-5 main ideas to focus on. For example, if your child is doing a report on elephants, he can focus on: 1) Appearance, 2) Diet, 3) Babies, 4) Behaviors.

3. Have your child find information on each of the 3-5 main ideas. He/she can write the information in point form notes. Make sure your child focuses on facts, data, and good detailed information. If needed, your child can organize the information in a graphic organizer.

4. Now, your child has enough information to write 3-5 paragraphs. Help your child to write a topic sentence for each paragraph. The topic sentences should introduce the paragraph's content. Then, he can take his point form notes and put them together in sentences.

5. After your child has the 3-5 paragraphs with good topic sentences, he/she should write a good, strong opening that tells the main idea of the report. A good opening can be a

question or very interesting fact. A strong opening sentence makes the reader want to read on.

6. A strong closing sentence or sentences finishes off the report. The closing should sum up the report and connect the main ideas together. It's almost like a summary of the report.

7. Finally, the fun part. Edit, edit, and edit. Have your child use an editing checklist.

8. When your child is finished, allow him/her to read the report out loud to family and/or friends.

Clearly, writing a report is not difficult once your child learns the proper organization and format. It is important for your child to add in facts and details. A report must have good factual information for the reader.

Report Writing
Grades 2-6

A **report** is a group of paragraphs with information about a topic. You must do some research to write a report.
You can look in books or go on the internet to find information for your topic.

Example:

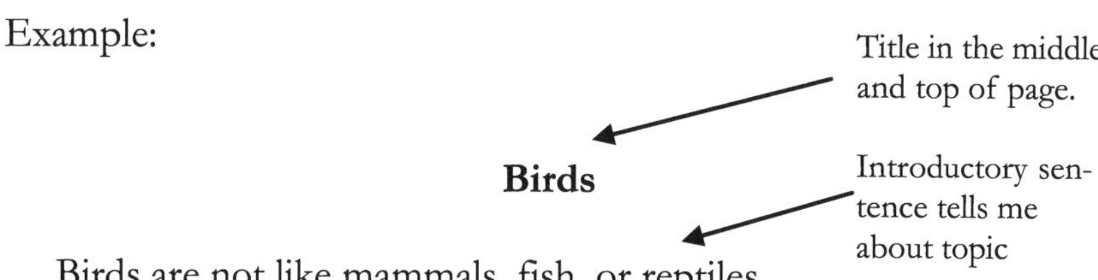

Birds

Birds are not like mammals, fish, or reptiles.

Birds have feathers. Their feathers come in different colors and sizes. Some feathers help keep birds warm and other feathers help birds fly. For example, the Snowy Owl has different feathers than a Bald Eagle.

Birds lay eggs inside their nests. Birds sit on their eggs to keep them warm. The eggs are made of hard shells that protect the babies until they are ready to hatch. The ostrich lays the largest eggs of all birds.

Birds have different diets. Falcons and hawks eat other birds and small mammals. Woodpeckers eat insects and acorns. Hummingbirds eat nectar from plants.

Birds are special animals. They are not like mammals or fish.

Conclusion

3 paragraphs
-feathers
-eggs
-food

Go to next page…

Use the following paragraphs and write them in the correct box on the next page. Photocopy the following graphic organizer so that it can be used again.

THESE PARAGRAPHS ARE NOT IN THE CORRECT ORDER

Mammals all have fur or hair. People are mammals and we have hair. Other mammals such as bears, rabbits and zebras have fur. The fur and hair help keep mammals warm. Mammals that live in the cold have thick fur.

Some mammals live in the water. Whales and dolphins are mammals that live in the ocean. They don't have fur or hair. Their skin is smooth, not scaly like a fish. Whales and dolphins breathe air like other mammals.

Mammals are different from other animals. Most mammal babies are born alive because most mammals don't lay eggs.

Mammals

Mammals have different diets. Some mammals, like lions are carnivores. They only eat meat. Rabbits and giraffes are mammals that eat plants. They are called herbivores. Bears and people are omnivores. Omnivores eat meat and plants.

Mammals are really different from other animals. We can live in the water or on land and we eat different foods. We are special!

Title
Introductory Sentence
1st Paragraph
2nd Paragraph
3rd Paragraph
Conclusion

Answers are on the next page…

Primary English: Writing Lesson: Writing a Report

Title
Mammals
Introductory sentence Mammals are different from other animals. Most mammal babies are born alive because most mammals don't lay eggs.
1st paragraph Mammals all have fur or hair. People are mammals and we have hair. Other mammals such as bears, rabbits and zebras have fur. The fur and hair help keep mammals warm. Mammals that live in the cold have thick fur.
2nd paragraph Some mammals live in the water. Whales and dolphins are mammals that live in the ocean. They don't have fur or hair. Their skin is smooth, not scaly like a fish. Whales and dolphins breathe air like other mammals.
3rd paragraph Mammals have different diets. Some mammals, like lions are carnivores. They only eat meat. Rabbits and giraffes are mammals that eat plants. They are called herbivores. Bears and people are omnivores. Omnivores eat meat and plants.
Conclusion Mammals are really different from other animals. We can live in the water or on land and we eat different foods. We are special!

Now write this report on another sheet of paper (or use the computer) in the correct format. See the next page.

Mammals

Mammals are different from other animals. Most mammal babies are born alive because most mammals don't lay eggs.

Mammals all have fur or hair. People are mammals and we have hair. Other mammals such as bears, rabbits and zebras have fur. The fur and hair help keep mammals warm. Mammals that live in the cold have thick fur.

Some mammals live in the water. Whales and dolphins are mammals that live in the ocean. They don't have fur or hair. Their skin is smooth, not scaly like a fish. Whales and dolphins breathe air like other mammals.

Mammals have different diets. Some mammals, like lions are carnivores. They only eat meat. Rabbits and giraffes are mammals that eat plants. They are called herbivores. Bears and people are omnivores. Omnivores eat meat and plants.

Mammals are really different from other animals. We can live in the water or on land and we eat different foods. We are special!

Informational Essays and Reports

An essay is a form of factual writing that is more than one paragraph in length. The key to writing a good informational essay or report is to be organized and understand the process and structure.

Prewriting

Starting Off

Before writing an informational essay, it is important to plan the 'who', 'what', and 'why'.

- It is important to know who or what you are writing about. Unless you are given a specific topic to write about, it is important to choose a topic that really interests you. If you are given a topic that does not necessarily interest you, find out if you can cover a subtopic or a topic related to the one that was given to you.

- Know who will be reading your report/essay. Will it be for your classmates, teacher, or community?
  Your vocabulary, facts, and overall writing should be dictated by your audience. That is, you wouldn't want to include difficult scientific concepts and vocabulary if your essay is to be read by other students.

- Lastly, how do you want your writing to sound? Do you want the essay to be very serious, funny, or scientific? The 'way' you write is sometimes just as important as 'what' you write. Your message will be understood according to the tone in your writing.

Putting it Together

What type of information do you plan on using? First, find reliable sources and determine important information. Once you have your information, find a focus. That is, specifically what aspect of the topic do you want to focus on? Then, organize your information into sub-categories. The rule of thumb is to use 3 main ideas in your essay and focus on each idea within their own paragraphs.

The 1st Draft

Remember, a good essay, like a story, must have a beginning, middle, and end.

Beginning
Your introductory paragraph should say something interesting or surprising in order to get the reader's attention. It should also introduce the subtopics you will be discussing in your essay.

Middle
The middle should include all of the ideas, facts, examples, and information about your topic. Each paragraph should contain a separate sub-topic and should be properly organized.

End
The final paragraph, or conclusion, should summarize the main points covered in your informational essay/report. It should also remind the reader what your main ideas were and why they were important.

Revising and Editing

Make sure that you have done the following in order to edit your writing:

1. Does my title identify my topic?

2. Have I introduced my topic in my introduction? Is my introduction interesting?
3. Are my paragraphs well organized (i.e. topic sentence, supporting sentences)?
4. Have I included facts, proof, and information that support my topic?
5. Will readers understand my writing (i.e. have I written to the correct audience)?
6. Have I edited my writing (i.e. grammar, punctuation, sentences)?

By staying organized and following the structure of an information essay/report, you will improve your chances for writing a well written essay.

Report Writing
Grades 4-8

The purpose of a **report** is to systematically organize factual information to classify and describe something. A **report** involves research to explore a topic.

A report has the following characteristics:

1. A title.
2. An opening sentence introducing the topic.
3. A body that usually contains at least 3 paragraphs. Each paragraph represents an idea.
4. A concluding statement.

How do I start?

1. Choose a topic that interests you. A specific topic is better than a general one (if you have a choice that is). For example, 'Fish' is too general and covers too many areas, but "The Puffer Fish" is specific enough for a report.

2. I will write 4 points I would like to learn and write about Puffer Fish.
   A) Appearance: What do they look like, how big are they?
   B) Special Features?
   C) Behaviour: What do they do? Puff up? Food?
   D) What is a Puffer Fish?

3. Now I will organize my 4 points in logical order.
   A) What is a Puffer Fish?
   B) Appearance
   C) Behaviour
   D) Special Features?

4. Now I will find information on the Internet, in books and magazines.
5. I will organize my information according to my 3 points. I can simply list my information or put it in a graphic organizer.

Point 1 – What is a Puffer Fish?
-also called the blowfish or globefish
-lives in tropical and subtropical waters
-over 120 different species of puffer fish
-related to porcupine fish
-second most poisonous vertebrate in the world

Point 2 – Appearance
-from 1 inch dwarf puffer to 3 feet long giant puffer
-can puff up because they have elastic skin and no ribs
-teeth sharp enough to cut off a human finger
-upper and lower jaws are fused together
-some puffer fish have spines on their skin

Point 3 – Behaviour
-inflates itself with water or air
-blend in with coral and live at bottom of ocean
-can turn themselves into a ball several times their size
-puffers are of few fish that can blink their eyes
-aggressive and guard territory
-can crack open shellfish with their beaks

Point 4 – Special Features
- 1 puffer fish has enough poison to kill 30 people
-they are a delicacy in Japan

6. I will write a topic sentence for each point.
A) Puffer fish are extremely poisonous fish that have unique abilities.
B) Puffer fish have some amazing features that allow them to survive.
C) Puffer fish can easily use their bodies to protect themselves.
D) Puffer fish have great defenses but they can still be eaten.

7. I will write an interesting introductory sentence. A question or a statement that makes people think is a good way to begin.
8. I will write a paragraph for each point.

9. I will write a closing paragraph that sums up my report.

10. I will edit my work.

You can make a graphic organizer like this one to organize your report. Take your point form notes and write them in the boxes.

Title Puffer Fish
Introductory Sentence and introductory paragraph Have you ever seen an animal blow itself up with air and water? Puffer fish are extremely poisonous fish that have unique abilities. Puffer fish are also known as blowfish or globefish and are related to the porcupine fish. There are over 120 different species of puffer fish. Puffer fish live in tropical and subtropical waters. They are the second most poisonous vertebrate in the world.
Point 1 Puffer fish have amazing features that allow them to survive. They can puff up in size because they have elastic skin and no ribs. Puffer fish range from the 1 inch dwarf puffer fish to the 3 foot giant puffer fish. The jaws of the puffer fish are fused together and their teeth are sharp enough to cut off a person's finger. Some puffers even have spines on their skin.

continued on the next page…

Point 2 *Puffer fish can easily use their bodies to protect themselves. They can inflate themselves into a ball several times their size by filling their bodies with air and water. Puffer fish can hide on the ocean floor because their colors help them blend in with the coral. They can be aggressive and guard their territory. Puffer fish use their sharp beaks to crack open shellfish.*
Point 3 *Puffer fish have great defenses but can still be eaten. One puffer fish has enough poison to kill 30 people. Even though they are deadly to humans, some people in Japan eat them. People who eat puffer fish can still die from the poison if the puffer fish isn't cut properly.*
Concluding sentence *Puffer fish are one of the most deadly animals on the planet. They bodies and behaviors have allowed them to adapt and survive.*

Go to the next page to see the final report

Puffer Fish

Have you ever seen an animal blow itself up with air and water?

Puffer fish are extremely poisonous fish that have unique abilities. Puffer fish are also known as blowfish or globefish and are related to the porcupine fish. There are over 120 different species of puffer fish. Puffer fish live in tropical and subtropical waters. They are the second most poisonous vertebrate in the world.

Puffer fish have amazing features that allow them to survive. They can puff up in size because they have elastic skin and no ribs. Puffer fish range from the 1 inch dwarf puffer fish to the 3 foot giant puffer fish. The jaws of the puffer fish are fused together and their teeth are sharp enough to cut off a person's finger. Some puffers even have spines on their skin.

Puffer fish can easily use their bodies to protect themselves. They can inflate themselves into a ball several times their size by filling their bodies with air and water. Puffer fish can hide on the ocean floor because their colors help them blend in with the coral. They can be aggressive and guard their territory. Puffer fish use their sharp beaks to crack open shellfish.

Puffer fish have great defenses but can still be eaten. One puffer fish has enough poison to kill 30 people. Even though they are deadly to humans, some people in Japan eat them. People who eat puffer fish can still die from the poison if the puffer fish isn't cut properly.

Puffer fish are one of the most deadly animals on the planet. They bodies and behaviors have allowed them to adapt and survive.

On the next page, you will find a graphic organizer that you can use when writing a report.

Title	
Introductory Sentence	
Point 1	
Point 2	
Point 3	
Concluding Sentence	

More Writing Tips

Cause and Effect Essay

What is a cause and effect essay?

Cause and effect essays discuss why things happen (causes) and what happens as a result (effects). Cause and effect is an effective way of organizing and ideas and determining their relationship. Explanation-type essays are based on cause and effect.

Follow these steps when writing a cause and effect essay

1. Determine the difference between a cause and the effect. To determine causes, ask, "Why did it happen?" To identify effects, ask, "What happened because of it?" For example:

   Cause
   The sidewalk was slippery.

   Effect
   You fell and hurt your leg.

   Often, when reading, you might find that several causes contribute to only one effect or several effects may result from only one cause.

   Causes
   The sidewalk was slippery.
   You weren't paying attention.
   You were wearing dress shoes.
   Effect
   You fell and hurt your leg.

When writing a cause and effect essay, it is best to map out all the possible causes and effects that are related to your subject. This is particularly important when writing an explanation (i.e. how something works like a bicycle or a volcano).

2. Create your thesis or opening statement. Make it clear to the reader whether you are discussing causes, effects, or both. Show your main idea right from the start. Most importantly, make sure that you use the words 'cause' and 'effect' when writing. This will make it clear to the reader right off the bat.
3. Make sure that your 'cause' is supported by the appropriate details. The reader should have a clear understanding of the cause and be able to follow it to the effects.
4. Use transition and linking words. Transition, or linking words, help weave the cause and effect together.

Linking words for causes:
because, due to, on cause is, another, since, for, first, second, because of

Linking words for effects:
consequently, as a result, thus, in the end, one result is, another is, therefore

Remember to do the following when writing a cause and effect essay:

1. Map out your cause(s) and effect(s).
2. Clearly indicate your opening statement in the beginning.
3. Support the 'cause(s)' with details.
4. Use linking words to show the relationship between cause and effect

Elementary Grades – Writing Skills

Elementary writing has so many aspects that it is difficult to sum them all up in one article. What's unique about elementary writing as opposed to the junior and intermediate (middle) grade writing curriculum is the fact that elementary writing is more skill based whereas the latter refines those skills.

Elementary writing is a cumulative process whereby young students build upon basic skills to more complex ones.

Let's take a look at the developmental process of elementary (grades 1-3) writing so that you, as a parent, have an idea as to how your child is learning to write. Of course, you may not know exactly *what* to help your child with (although you can always go online to look at your child's state or provincial curriculum), but you can get an idea as to what to look for when your child comes home with a piece of writing. Take a look at the following to get a better idea:

- **Sentences** – This first basic skill an elementary student learns is how to write sentences. Students are first taught the mechanics of writing a sentence such as capitalizing the first word and adding a period. The next skill they will learn is to create different sentence types (declarative, question, exclamatory, etc…). While doing so, students will learn the appropriate punctuation for each type of sentence.

- **Classifying and Organizing -** After students learn how to write sentences, they will learn how to classify and organize the sentence according to the piece of writing. For example, students will learn how to organize a simple procedure (e.g. making a sandwich) and organize their ideas (e.g. sorting ideas through pictures or charts).

- **Research –** In the elementary grades, students will also learn how to find simple information and use that information in their writing (e.g. find information on lions and write the information in a simple report).

- **Personal Experiences and Reflections -** Students will also learn how to write a journal where they express their feelings about a subject and they will also learn how to recount events in their lives.

- **Forms –** Elementary students will also be exposed to the various forms of writing. For example, younger students will be introduced to the format of: *descriptive writing, explanations, recounts, letter writing, paragraph writing, persuasive writing, procedures, reports, and personal narratives.*

- **Style -** Students will begin to learn the basics of writing styles. These are the skills that will be developed in greater detail when students enter the junior and intermediate (middle) grades. Students will learn how to develop a writing voice, choosing descriptive verbs and adjectives, and develop sentence fluency (i.e. the readability of sentences).

By knowing what your child is learning in writing class, you will be able to monitor and help your child become a better writer.

How to Write a Conclusion

Writing a conclusion is similar to writing a paragraph.

The first sentence in a conclusion is the topic sentence. It should be the most important sentence in your conclusion. Your first sentence in your conclusion must contain the main idea of your entire report.

The following sentence in your conclusion reiterates the main ideas from each paragraph. Your introduction 'introduced' your main ideas that were stated in your paragraph and your conclusion reiterates those main ideas. Essentially, you have (hopefully) given proof for your main ideas in your paragraphs, so, you can confidently state the ideas again as fact in your conclusion.

Your conclusion should be written in the following order:

1. Your first sentence must state the main idea of your entire piece of work.
2. The next few sentences should support your main idea by reiterating the main ideas from each paragraph.
3. The last sentence should be similar to the first sentence except that it should be in your own words. It should be **your** summary of the conclusion. For example, let's say you did a report on sharks. If your first sentence in the conclusion stated, "Sharks are efficient predators." your last sentence can be something like, "Sharks are clearly the king of the ocean." This sentence supports that fact that sharks are efficient predators because it states their superiority as a species.

It is important to remember to organize your concluding paragraph much like any other paragraph.

Ideas – Writing Ideas for Various Writing Genres

Writing ideas are sometimes hard to come by. It is easy for most students to start to find information, but it is difficult for them to decide on an idea unless they are given a specific one from their teacher.

Students should choose a topic based on the type of writing assignment. For example, a topic for a report is quite different than that of an explanation.

The following 5 types of writing each have their own unique topics. They are:

- Explanatory
- Persuasive
- Descriptive
- Narrative
- Procedural

Explanatory

- **Causes** - volcanoes, erosion, hatred, tornadoes, pollution, war
- **Different Kinds of...** - movies, stores, cities, clothes, music, TV shows, villains
- **Definitions** - family, fear, friends, culture

Persuasive

- **Persuading** - homework is bad, stealing is wrong, seat belts, too much TV, video games are fun, gum should be allowed in school, pets should have rights

Descriptive

- **Places** - your home, city, country, zoo, forest, store, kitchen, lake, farm
- **People** - friend, teacher, hero, family member, famous athlete, singer, actor
- **Things** - pet, bicycle, video game, car, food, book, hobby

Narrative

- **Fiction** - fantasy story, historical fiction, romance, science fiction, realistic fiction,
- **Essay** - being happy, being a good friend, learning, volunteering

Procedural

- **How to... -** bake a cake, exercise, save money, how to vote, fix something, teach something, take care of a pet

Of course, there are many, many more ideas out there for each category. What's important for students though, is to choose (if they are able to) a topic which they are interested in, then, they can decide on the type of writing. Or, if a student is required to do a type of writing (e.g. an explanation), then they can decide upon a topic of interest.

More Writing Ideas

Students often find it difficult to develop writing ideas. Unless students are given a specific topic with specific sub-topics, students can spend a great deal of time deciding what to write about.

Good writing ideas come from many sources. It requires more than just sitting around thinking of an idea or surfing the internet. There are several ways to generate good ideas for writing.

Regardless of whether it is an essay, an informative report, or science report, good ideas will make all writing assignments stand out above the rest.

Here are some ways that you can generate good writing ideas:

- **Reflect upon personal experiences**. Have you been to specific places? Have you seen interesting things? Use your personal background knowledge and experiences in order to come up with ideas. For example, assume you have to write a report on a specific cultural aspect of a country. Which country? What cultural aspect? Perhaps your grandparents come from England and you enjoy soccer. There's an idea! You can write a report on the cultural impact of soccer on the English economy (for example). The point here is for you to find something that you can relate to. This will help you generate ideas and it might make the project more interesting.

- **Read stories, books, and magazines on a topic you are interested in.** By reading books and stories about personally interesting topics, you can get more ideas and gain different perspectives. For example, assume you like computers. You already have a good knowledge of home computers. Let's say you read a magazine story about a new kind of home computer or a new application or program. Having read the article on a topic that interests you, you've just stumbled upon a new idea for a report or essay.

- **Talk to friends and family.** Sometimes friends and family know you better than you know yourself. Assume you have no idea what to write about. Your parent or friend can remind you about something you did, somewhere you went, or some interest you have had in the past that you forgot about. Or, they might simply come up with a great idea for you. Don't be shy, ask others.

- **Go Online.** It's unbelievable how visiting one site about a topic can lead you somewhere completely different. You can get on the internet, have a specific topic in mind, and within a few minutes, find yourself reading about an interesting topic that has nothing to do with the first website you visited.

- **Create a topic web.** Let's say you are interested in cars, for example. Write the word 'car' in the middle of a blank page and circle it. Draw lines from the circle with 'cars' in it to create other words and put them in circles. The other words must have something to do with cars. For example, you may have written down the word 'Ferrari', or 'engine'. Then, from the words 'Ferrari' and 'engine', draw lines to other related words until you create a word web. By the time you get to the edge of the paper, you may have such words as 'Indy 500', or 'Solar Powered Cars'. This is a great way to generate ideas from your areas of interest.

Having good writing ideas will help your child create informative and interesting pieces of writing. Try as many methods above as you can in order to generate a good writing idea.

Improving Writing through Conventions

What are conventions?

Conventions are the fancy educational word for the 'mechanical' correctness of writing.

This refers to the proper spelling, paragraphing, the use of capitals, punctuation, and overall grammatical structure (pretty much everything besides the actual content).

A good piece of writing consists of two major components. The first is obviously the content of the work (i.e. the message, the story, or the facts). The second is the structure of the writing (i.e. the conventions). Students can improve their writing skills (specifically regarding conventions) through practice. They must consistently proofread and edit their writing with care (and not rely so much on a word processing program). Since the improper use of conventions disrupts the flow of the writing, it thus has an effect on the message (which we know is part of the content).

After your child writes his/her rough draft of a piece of writing, review the following tips in order to check for the correct use of conventions.

- Make sure spelling is correct. Students shouldn't completely rely on word processors because word processors do not always take in account the 'context' of the word (therefore the word processor might give a homonym, which may be the incorrect word in the particular context).

- Students should have a thorough understanding of the rules of capitalization, quotation marks, grammar, and paragraphing.

- Make sure that your child's writing conventions are at grade level (you can easily go online to see the curriculum standards for your child...simply search for your child's state/province and 'curriculum').

- Give your child an editing checklist and have him/her choose 1 convention at a time to check. For example, assume your child is ready to edit. Have him/her start off using a green pen or pencil crayon to check all capitals. Then, use a blue pen or pencil to correct all spelling mistakes, and so on. It is important to use different colors compartmentalize each convention when making corrections.

You can use these strategies to help develop your child's writing skills and improve his/her use of conventions.

Linking and Transition Words

Sentences and paragraphs must be organized so that the reader can easily follow the information from one sentence to the next, and more importantly, from one paragraph to the next.

Transition, or linking words, allow writers to connect sentences and paragraphs. Transition or linking words can indicate the **time order**, **place order**, and **order of importance**.

Time Order

When writing, it is extremely important to indicate the chronological (time) order of events otherwise the reader will be confused as to when everything happened.

Some **time order** linking words are:

about, after, before, during, first, second, third, today, tomorrow, yesterday, next, soon, after, finally, then, and *as soon as*

Place Order

When writing a descriptive or expository paragraph or essay, students should use place order linking words. Place order linking words describe where things are located.

Some **place order** linking words are:

above, across, along, around, behind, below, beside, between, by, down, in front of, in back of, inside, outside, near, over, left, right, under

Order of Importance

News stories and essays should be organized in order of importance. That is, the most important information should be given first. Students should use this concept when writing persuasive and expository essays. Sometimes, writers like to save the most important point for last as well.

Some **order of importance** words are:

for this reason, in fact, for instance, as a result, therefore, in conclusion, firstly, most importantly, secondly, on the other hand, however, in summary,

Students should use these linking words to begin a paragraph and sentence when writing.

<u>More on Transition Words</u>

In a personal narrative or recount, the reader has to know when things happen and in what order. Understanding the order of events helps the reader organize the information.

Transition words help the reader know the time order of events in a piece of writing. Some examples of transition words are: during, after, next, then, and before.

It is important for writers to use transition words not only to show the time order, but to separate the events. The transition words help the reader break up the events so that they are not meshed together.

Your child can use the following writing cues in order to practice time order and transition words for longer pieces of writing (e.g. personal narratives and recounts).

- Your child can write a sentence that could be from one of his/her personal narratives. Your child can replace a word with a transition word at the beginning of the sentence.

- Your child can write a sentence about a recent experience and use a transition word to start it off.

- Your child can write two sentences using a transition word to connect the two ideas. The second idea should begin with a transition word.

- Your child can practice using transition words by writing a retell of his/her day (not all the details from the day are needed, only a handful of main events). The retell should include several transition words that connect the events in time order.

My Child Doesn't Like to Write

It isn't easy to motivate students to write if they are not interested. Quite often, unmotivated students see writing as a chore as opposed to a form of self expression.

They key to motivating your child to write is to focus on the content as opposed to the form. If you can get your child interested in writing for the sake of writing, he/she will ultimately develop the appropriate skills later on.

You can help motivate your child to write by trying some of the following:

1. Reward your child for completing any writing activities whether it is at school or at home. Rewards such as praise, movie, or extra video or TV time are good ideas. You know your child best.

2. Have your child create personal stories about topics of interest. For example, if your child likes a certain movie, sport, video game, or TV show, have him/her write a story about his or her topic of interest. Your child can include him or herself in the story. Let your child make it silly, funny, or any way (within reason) he or she wishes. Your child is more likely to try to be successful when writing about something of interest.

3. Encourage your child to read his or her stories to family members. There's nothing like positive reinforcement, encouragement, and praise from loved ones. Your child will develop a sense of pride and accomplishment.

4. My favorite suggestion is to have your child type out his/her story on the computer (or a family member can do the typing if it is difficult for the child). Your child can learn how to use spell check, and, for added story writing fun, your child can paste pictures into a program such as Microsoft PowerPoint to make a slide show to accompany his or her story. This is a great way to get your child interested in writing. He/she will have a slide

show (which is like a movie) that will give him/her a visual representation of the story.
This is great when your child writes about anything from superheroes to science fiction stories.

Wait until your child has developed an interest in writing until you decide to work on his/her writing skills. Once your child begins writing on a regular basis, you will have overcome the motivation issue and could then begin working on writing skills.

Point of View

Students often have difficulty keeping a consistent point of view when writing essays. It is common to find a student start writing in the first person then switch over to the third person point of view.

First Person Point of View (I)

- It is easy for the author to use his or her own voice and perspective
- Easy for the author to add description and emotion because the author is part of the story
- Good to use when writing a narrative story
- Not a good choice when writing factual essays (i.e. reports for example should not contain opinions)
- Good for personal narratives/recounts

Second Person Point of View (You)

- Good to use when giving instructions for procedure writing
- Not a good choice when writing narratives nor reports (rarely used in fiction)

Third Person Point of View (He/She/They)

- Allows the author to separate him or herself from the action in a narrative
- Excellent point of view choice when writing factual information (e.g. reports, explanations)
- A better choice for better writers

The Writing Process

Your child comes home with a writing assignment and you're not sure where to start. Sometimes students are given graphic organizers in order to help them with their writing assignments and other times they are on their own. Regardless of the type of writing assignment, your child should approach his/her work in an organized fashion. Some students are able to whip up a report or procedure with their eyes closed but for the rest of the class, well, they need guidance. The 'Writing Process' is a systematic way that increases a student's chances on becoming a good writer. This process incorporates every aspect of planning, writing, organizing, and editing a piece of writing. It's very much like the sculptor who starts off with a mental picture, uses his chisel to shape his work, and finally does the last bit of fine detail.

You can help your child become a better writer by using the 'Writing Process'.

1. **Prewriting** – Decide on a topic and organize ideas. Figure out the purpose for the writing (i.e. who is the intended audience?) and choose the correct format.
2. **Drafting** – Write a rough draft (or rough copy). Create a good 'hook' to get the reader's attention and focus on ideas rather than the mechanics of writing (that will be later on).
3. **Revising** – Share the writing with friends or family members in order to get feedback and make changes.
4. **Editing** – Like the sculptor who smoothes out the fine lines, your child must proofread his work very carefully. He can use a checklist and/or have others proofread.
5. **Publishing** - Publish the writing using the appropriate form (e.g. word processor, fonts, graphics, titles, etc…).

Have your child follow the 'Writing Process' every time he/she has a writing assignment. By following each stage of the process, your child will ensure that he/she becomes a better writer. It all comes down to, practice, organization, details, and effort.

Word Choice

The choice of words your child uses is critical for optimal writing. Having a strong vocabulary is essential for your child to convey meaning. The variety of words that are used in a piece of writing create a rich and colorful form of communication that involves the reader. Good word choice clarifies, illustrates, and expands ideas. The focus of good word choice skills is not to impress the reader (or teacher) with a strong vocabulary; rather, it provides the writer with a more rounded use of everyday words. Students should focus on using proper words in the correct context. After your child writes his/her rough draft of a piece of writing, review the following tips in order to improve his/her choice of words.

- The words are specific and used in the correct context (e.g. instead of , "He walked down the road," we can write, "He casually sauntered down the road,")
- Words should 'strike' the reader's eyes and remain in their minds.
- The sentences should be natural and appropriate for the reader (i.e. is the writing intended for an adult, teen…? Is the reader a teacher or someone else?)
- Use lively verbs (e.g. instead of 'ran away' we could write 'darted off') to add energy to the text.
- Incorporate colorful adjectives in order to paint a better picture.
- Use a thesaurus or a word processor 'synonym' tool.
- Don't try too hard. Difficult words and an over abundance of colorful adjectives can easily tire out a reader.

You can use these strategies to help your child to create an engaging piece of writing that clearly conveys a message in an interesting and natural way.

Writing Basics

Before embarking on a journey with the written word, there are four writing concepts that you must be aware of.

1. **Finding a Topic –** Unless your teacher has given you a specific topic, you should write about anything that interests you! When you write about a topic that interests you, you will be more involved and motivated to do a better job. Finding information and creating the text will be more appealing because if the topic is of interest to you, it will be more engaging. For example, assume your teacher said you had to do a report on Ancient Greek culture and history doesn't interest you. But... you enjoy watching the Olympics on television. Perfect! You can do a report on the history of the Olympics. The key here is to ***find*** a topic of interest.

2. **Find Your Information and a Focus** – If you are writing a personal narrative, you just need your own brain because in order to write a personal narrative, you only need your past experiences. If, on the other hand, you are writing a report, you must find reliable sources. Once you have found the sources, decide on your focus. It's easy to get lost in the huge amount of information that's out there. For example, let's say you were writing a science report on the human body. You certainly wouldn't want to write about the entire human body (after all, it takes medical students years to read all that stuff!), instead, focus on one specific aspect of the human body, for example, the eye. The key here is to find a specific topic ***within*** a topic (granted your teacher allows you to do so).

3. **Make an Outline and Write Your First Draft –** It's really important to create a graphic organizer (i.e. a chart) to plan your writing assignment. Organize the topic sentences, the paragraphs, and the conclusion. Once you have your writing organized, you can start on your first draft. When

writing the first draft, don't bother worrying about spelling or grammar. It's more important to organize your ideas and make sure that your information is relevant and in proper order.

4. **Editing** - When your first draft is done, you should start editing. Use the spellchecker in your word processor and a good old fashioned dictionary. Use an online thesaurus to make your words more descriptive and lively. Obtain an editing checklist to go over grammar and punctuation mistakes. Make sure you read your writing out loud to catch your own errors. Finally, have other people read over your work and help you edit it.

Follow these 4 writing basics in order to become a successful writer.

Conclusion

I recommend that your child practices the lessons in this book in accordance with his or her studies in school. Don't over-do it. Try to make your child's at home writing meaningful by having it relate to the writing skills your child is learning at school at that time.

The tips that accompany the lessons will help you, the parent, to understand *how* to help your child. I suggest that you re-read the concepts prior to helping your child at home with each specific skill.

The last section contains writing tips that don't fit in with the lesson section but are still quite important for your child to know.

Use the templates or create your own. They are excellent tools to help your child stay organized when writing essays.

I know that this book will help you help your child improve his or her writing.

Persistence and consistency are the keys to success.

Printed in Great Britain
by Amazon